First edition for the United States and Canada © copyright 2002 by Barron's Educational Series, Inc.

First edition for Great Britain published 2001 by Hodder Wayland,
an imprint of Hodder Children's Books

All inquiries should be addressed to:
Barron's Educational Series, Inc.
250 Wireless Boulevard
Hauppauge, NY 11788
http://www.barronseduc.com

Library of Congress Catalog Card No. 2001093217

ISBN-13:978-0-7641-2119-7

Date of Manufacture : January 2015
Manufactured by : Shenzhen Wing King Tong Paper Products Co. Ltd.,
Shenzhen, Guangdong, China.

Printed in China
20 19 18 17 16 15 14 13

My Amazing Body

A FIRST LOOK AT HEALTH AND FITNESS

PAT THOMAS
ILLUSTRATED BY LESLEY HARKER

BARRON'S

You have an amazing body.

So do all the other people
in the world.

You have a brain that can do more complicated thinking than any computer.

You have a body that can move in more different ways than any robot.

You have five senses – sight, hearing, taste, touch, and smell – that tell you lots of important things about the world around you without you even having to ask.

Your body can do lots of other things on its own, too. Your heart beats, your lungs breathe –

and when you graze your knee or get a cold, your body can make you well again without you having to tell it to.

But your body can't do
everything on its own.
It needs some help
from you.

There are lots of ways you can help your body stay fit and healthy. All of them are easy and most of them are fun as well.

What about you?

How many different things can you think of that help keep your body healthy? How often do you do these things?

Food contains vitamins, minerals,
and energy. These things
help you to think and
play and grow.

14

When you eat fresh fruits and vegetables
and protein foods like meat, milk,
and beans you are giving your
body the things it
needs to grow.

But when you eat lots
of sweets, chips, and
soft drinks you are
not giving your
body the vitamins
it needs.

These foods and drinks may taste nice, but if you have them too often your body may become sick.

It's OK to eat these foods sometimes. But the best way to stay healthy is to eat lots of different kinds of foods every day.

Another way to help your body is to use it in every way you can. That means getting lots of exercise. Exercise helps your muscles stay strong and fit and helps your bones grow.

When you are running and jumping and stretching you are exercising your heart and helping it to pump blood all over your body. You are also exercising your lungs, helping them to breathe in more air.

What about you?

Do you like to run and jump around?
What are your favorite types of exercise?
How often do you get to do these things?

There are other good ways
to help your body
stay healthy.

When you bathe and brush your teeth you are
helping keep yourself clean and free from germs.

And while exercising
is good, resting is
important, too.

We all need plenty of sleep and to have times
when we can work or play quietly.

Your body is always giving you clues about what it needs.

When your body needs rest, you feel tired.

When your body needs food, you feel hungry.

And when your body has had enough food, you feel full.

When you feel a pain it's a message that a part of you needs care and attention. It's important to listen to the messages your body is sending you.

Even healthy people get ill sometimes. It's never fun to get sick, but when you are sick your body is doing something amazing.

It is making a memory of that illness, so that next time
you can get better more quickly.

You only have one body and it is the most important thing you will ever own.

Your body is built
to last you a long time. And if
you take really good care of it, it will.

FURTHER INFORMATION

Children often imitate adults when it comes to eating habits. If parents are rarely seen eating fresh fruits and vegetables or freshly prepared meals, children will learn that this is the correct way to eat. Prepackaged foods are convenient but are often nutritionally poor. As often as is practical, parents should strive to put fresh food on the table. Likewise, children usually copy their parents' exercise habits. To encourage your child to get up and move, you may have to do the same. Special activities for children such as Saturday soccer or swimming are great. But regular activities that all the family can enjoy are also a good way of encouraging your child to be active.

There is an argument that, for small children, several small meals throughout the day is a better way to maintain health and absorb nutrients since it places less stress on the digestive system. While there is a place in most diets for crackers and candy, these need to be balanced by healthier alternatives. A well-chosen snack can also ward off the extreme hunger that can lead to continual cravings and bingeing on the wrong kinds of foods. Often children will eat whatever is around, so it's best to make sure there is always a bowl of colorful fruit on hand for children to choose from.

Food fads and a decreased appetite are normal during childhood. As your child's growth slows down, appetite will also decline. Although it may seem that your child is not eating enough, it is highly unlikely that your child's appetite will decrease to such an extent that health is compromised. At some point during the pre-school years, many children go through another growth spurt. Take advantage of your child's increased appetite at this time and introduce a greater variety of healthier food options based on freshly prepared dishes and unprocessed whole foods.

Schools may be well suited to teach about diet and fitness from many different angles. Exploring different religious customs that involve food or finding out about the foods people from other cultures eat can broaden children's horizons considerably. Similarly, introducing a wide range of physical education or playground activities can aid children in finding a sport that suits them. Some schools have found that introducing a "snack time" in the afternoon is influential. Once children leave preschool they often don't have an afternoon break of this nature. A ten-minute break in the afternoon for the class to snack on healthy foods can improve energy levels and help to reinforce good eating habits.

GLOSSARY

Nutrients The vitamins and minerals in your food are known as nutrients. These are the things your body needs to grow and stay healthy.

Energy Energy is the fuel that makes your body work properly. Your food provides the energy that powers your brain, your muscles, and all the other parts of your body.

Germs Germs are living things that are too small to see. They don't usually cause problems to you. If you are not strong because you are eating the wrong foods or not getting enough sleep, then it is possible that the germs could cause you to become sick.

USEFUL CONTACTS

American Dietetic Association
216 W. Jackson Boulevard
Chicago, IL 60606-6995
(312) 899-0040
http://www.eatright.org

The Vegetarian Resource Group
P.O. Box 1463, Dept. IN
Baltimore, MD 21203
(410) 366-VEGE
http://www.vrg.org

BOOKS TO READ

Nonfiction
Children's Book of Yoga
by Thia Luby (Clear Light, 1998)

Get Moving: Tips on Exercise (Your Health Series)
by Kathy Feeney (Bridgestone Books, 2001)

Good Enough to Eat: A Kid's Guide to Food and Nutrition
by Lizzy Rockwell (HarperCollins, 1999)

Healthy Cooking for Kids: Building Blocks for a Lifetime of Good Nutrition
by Shelly Null and Gary Null (Griffin Trade Paperback, 1999)

Quick Meals for Healthy Kids and Busy Parents: Wholesome Family Recipes in 30 Minutes or Less from Three Leading Child Nutrition Experts
by Sandra K. Nissenberg, Margaret L. Bogle, and Audrey C. Wright (John Wiley, 1995)

Fiction
Fly Trap by Anastasio/Cooper (G & D, 1997)

From Head to Toe
by Eric Carle (HarperCollins, 1999)

Oliver's Fruit Salad by Vivian French (Orchard Books, 1998)

Pooh's Little Fitness Book
by A. A. Milne (Dutton, 1996)

The Very Hungry Caterpillar by Eric Carle (Penguin Putnam, 1994)